How to Become Invisible

How to Become Invisible

Poems by

Mary McCarthy

© 2023 Mary McCarthy. All rights reserved.
This material may not be reproduced in any form, published,
reprinted, recorded, performed, broadcast,
rewritten or redistributed without
the explicit permission of Mary McCarthy.
All such actions are strictly prohibited by law.

Cover image painted by Mary McCarthy
Cover design by Shay Culligan

ISBN: 978-1-63980-477-1

Kelsay Books
502 South 1040 East, A-119
American Fork, Utah 84003
Kelsaybooks.com

To my sister, Dorothy, who never let me go.

Acknowledgments

Versions of these poems appeared in the following publications:

The Awakenings Review: "Talk, Talk, Talk"

Earth's Daughters: "Enthralled," "Incendiary," "Invitation"

The Ekphrastic Review: "Burn"

Evening Street Review: "ECT the Curing"

Gnarled Oak: "Saving Face," "Skins"

Incandescent Mind: "Metamorphoses and Mood Swings"

Mindful: "The Madwoman as Apostate"

Poetry Circle Forum: "Outsiders," "That Last Time in the Hospital"

Silver Birch Press: "How to Become Invisible"

Third Wednesday: "Crow Song"

Verse-Virtual: "Stolen," "Bad Medicine," "They Should Have Known," "Wild Night," "Aftershock"

Visual Verse: "Irresistible"

White Pelican Review: "After So Much ECT"

Contents

Misfit	13
How to Become Invisible	14
They Should Have Known	15
Metamorphoses and Mood Swings	16
Challenges	17
You Wake	18
Symptoms	19
Depression	20
Devil I Know	21
Outsiders	22
Seeing in the Dark	23
Incendiary	24
Talk Talk Talk	25
Wild Night	26
Break	27
Blessed	28
Irresistible	29
Burn	30
Back to Zero	31
Since the Fall	32
All the Wrong Moves	33
Unfit	34
Quick Fix/Emergency Room	35
Dear Doctor	36
Medication	37
Bad Medicine	38
Strangers So Unkind	40
ECT the Curing	41
Aftershock	42
After So Much ECT	43
After Shock	44
That Last Time in the Hospital	45
The Madwoman as Apostate	46

Skins	48
Saving Face	49
Imposter	50
Ghost	51
Crow Song	52
Stolen	54
Vision	55
Enthralled	56
Your Apology, Dear Friend	58
Invitation	59

Misfit

Before we start
I have to punch a few holes
in normal
just to let some air in
just so I can breathe
while you unpack
the rules and expectations
measuring me for a box
that won't be big enough
and shoes that won't fit.

Where I come from
madness was often
a sort of gift
not rare enough
to scare anyone away.
Here I spend too much time
watching the doors close
behind you.

How to Become Invisible

Lose your job, your mind, your husband
step over the lines, off the map,
into unmarked alleys

Talk too fast, too much, too loud,
or not at all

Balk at the strangeness
of ordinary things
spot the dark intent behind
their bland disguises

Walk too close to the edge
of every conversation
answer the words behind the words they say

Forget to smile, to wash, to comb your hair
wear your clothes carelessly

Count the rough stitches
where the patchwork world
threatens separation

Carry your ghosts with you
shuffling and mumbling
in a long procession
that follows you down the street

Where no one sees you now
you've lost your place
your face your reflection

And even your shadow
fades to nothing
in the unrelenting sun

They Should Have Known

I was trouble
when at three I threw a tantrum
because the sun set
Should have known I'd be
always at odds with the real
so obstinate in my refusal
of the usual
they feared I might someday
deny the law of gravity
and lose touch with more
than sanity
unlock my grip
on the earth itself
and come untethered
like a loose balloon
flying out of reach

Metamorphoses and Mood Swings

Sometimes I am Byzantine, winged
and intricate as an insect, a mantid
with many jointed legs,
hard and jeweled as a beetle
soft as a moth.
Sometimes I am sad, muddled
and formless, tired and full of rain.
My tears flow endlessly down,
a salty river,
where, like a new Ophelia,
I barely keep afloat,
and nothing can reach me.
Sometimes I fly, like a steel
needle, through air clean
and sharp as a cut. I feel
everything at once, elbow deep
in trees, their leaves caress
my face, and I can feel their roots
curl in the earth.
Sometimes I am too fast
for anyone to catch, I can do
and do more than I ever
could before. I go beyond
the need for sleep, inventing
unusual uses for every hour.
And sometimes I am far too tired
to be anyone, to walk or speak
or think. So I shut down
and send them all
home with a note
that I won't be back until the next
resurrection.

Challenges

You can't prepare
for catastrophe
the way you studied for exams
and practiced conversations
Sane enough to pass.

Assume nothing will stay
the way it is for long.
Change is the only rule
you can be sure of.
No matter how we try
to force now
into yesterday's old clothes
it will always be an unexpected
stranger
coming at you quick
as a bullet
you must catch in your teeth.

You Wake

And the world has been replaced
by its own drab shadow.
Not trees but their flat
cardboard imitations
no birds but crows
ink black against a white sky.
They have swallowed the sun
the way a snake
swallows an egg
taking down the future
in one smooth gulp.
You stare back
with eyes so dry
they can't close
on the world stripped
to bone and ash,
even the oceans gone
leaving the earth behind.

Symptoms

I can't read.
The words go on and on
under my eyes, but they refer
to nothing I can imagine.
I might as well
sit with a text in Arabic
and at least admire
the shapes the words make
on the page. That way
there would be no question
of meaning between us.
My hands lie curled up
in my lap. If I open them
it is only to stare
at the nothing I keep there.
Surely somewhere there is a map
for this place. I have found myself
here often enough,
But I can't remember the way
in or out. Everyone talks at me
from behind a mask.
The voices,
disembodied, could belong
to anyone. I taste fear bright
as metal on my tongue.

Depression

Rising quietly at first,
it brushes me with a soft wing,
darkness like the echo of some
final cry,
sadness like the taste of cold
iron, salt on my lips,
tears rising hot and bitter
to blur my sight.
Suddenly all is lost and I stand
hopeless again in the litter
of my days; nothing can save me
from the nothing in my heart.
I can light candles, cook dinner,
iron clothes and wash the floors,
it doesn't matter.
What you see is the event horizon
of a black hole.
There will be no escape
from its terrible gravity,
swallowing my life as
fast as I live it.

Devil I Know

Trying to hold it off
I work hard
cleaning what's already clean
cooking food no one will eat
stalling thought
with puzzles
reading books
I can't remember
from one page to the next
leaving no space
for even one long breath.
One small crack
in these flimsy walls
and the suffocating dark
rushes in
taking up every inch
until there's not enough
left of me
to try again
too far from everything
In a room without air
where I won't last for long.

Outsiders

Not everyone can suffer
politely.
Some pain is clumsy

ugly as the troll
squatting in cold mud
under a lovely bridge.

I can't blame you
for looking up,
some frogs just can't be

kissed to transformation.
Like tricks that fail to convince
they embarrass

by staying what they are,
sad reminders
of how very little

magic you command.
Some suffering just makes you itch,
declaring itself like a bad rash,

irritating until it does
the only thing you can forgive
and fades away.

Not everyone gets over it
beats the odds
has no regrets-

some of us just
howl in the wasteland
outside the reach of grace.

Seeing in the Dark

This is not a room
but a bowl you can't climb out of,
a tunnel with no end.
Shadow on shadow, so black
it makes your eyes ache,
sends your heart skittering,
wild to escape, where nothing
breaks like morning
at the world's edge.
This is the dark answer
to your worst suspicions,
ringing with echoes
of unfamiliar voices
that won't show their faces
or stop their dull mutter,
going on and on until
your eyes invent
something to see-
a kaleidoscope of splintered light
cold as witchfire
spinning lies you can't believe
as you try to make yourself
as small as possible
so small and still
the great white owl
with her silent wings
and reaching claws
won't find you.

Incendiary

Today not blood
but something far
more volatile
fizzes in my veins
my thoughts ignite
and burn like sparklers
held by children
waiting for the great
novas and explosions
coming on full dark

I turn and turn again
a spinning wheel
a fountain magnifying fire
I strobe like heat lightning
at the edge of your attention
until I run out of gravity
and collapse
flaring like an incandescent star

tomorrow may be
all ember and ash
but tonight might throw off
heat enough to last
through one more dark forever

Talk Talk Talk

It's a simple conversation
until I join it.
Then, helpless,
I watch myself
effervescing
like an Alka Seltzer tablet
in a glass of plain water.
I see it but can't
stop it.
Once tipped over the rim
it has to drop
until it hits bottom
and foams itself away
into nothing but salt
and a bitter taste.
I try to swallow,
hoping no one will remember
my foolish tizzy
the crazy words coming
too fast, too full
of puns and rhymes, rising
like bubbles to dissolve
against the walls
of your silence.

Wild Night

Chased out of sleep
by a flaming tiger
roaring down at me
like a golden comet
getting close enough
to singe my hair
and put a hot kiss
on my neck
sure to leave a scar
that won't fade
when he drives me out
into the next day
with its dull safety
the familiar chain
of hours in step
like soldiers
all the same
making me turn back
to look over my shoulder
remembering his
breathtaking
wild disorder
sweet and dangerous
a fatal glory
so real I can still
taste it

Break

After the last apocalypse
I shine, radioactive,
outlawed, expelled,
ungrammatical,
left alone
where no angels come
where crows have more mercy,
bringing only a keen appetite
and not a burning sword.

Crows suit me well,
their polished blacks a comfort
to eyes tired of staring into fire.
Quiet now,
kneeling in the cinders
of my burnt out star,
I drag a finger
through rough ash
trying to remember how
to write my name.

Blessed

Angels never come to me
with comfort.
They split the air
with visions
bright and dangerous
as the sun's halo
in a full eclipse,
catching me
in a foolish stare
that will leave me blind.

Soon I see nothing
but these incandescent
shadows
flaring up at me,
the world like a charcoal fire
sprayed with gasoline
burning me
and everything I touch
with a glory
more than human
flesh can bear.

Irresistible

No way to stop it
a sudden eruption
hot as the first explosion
of everything from nothing
atom to infinity
in no time at all
swinging me into
my next tsunami
an exponential rush
of energy and light
brighter than any sun
generating storms
wild enough to carry
worlds away
and burn them all to ash-

in rivers of incandescent plasma
I dance in my red boots
over all objections
unregulated
free as god
in his unreachable orbit
I ride joy
like an unbroken horse
a rocket launched
into the darkness
that surrounds us all

Burn

When the gate drops
when the storm takes you
so high and far
all your ordinary days
shrink to insignificance
while the stars spin out
of their orbits
and you break free of gravity
rising like a new sun
spinning in the glory
of your own
inexhaustible fires
your heat expanding
until your farthest atoms
brush up against
the rim of the universe
where time and matter
took their first steps
out of the great nothing-

and you can only hold on
to your wild exaltation
even though this isn't
your first time
and like the bull rider
you know the end will find you
thrown to the dust
torn flesh and broken bones
hard payment for that brief
ecstasy

Back to Zero

Bad as you knew it was
you couldn't have imagined this
Still holding on
your fingers curled into claws
all energies bent
to keeping your place
the one you fought
so hard for
the one you thought
you couldn't lose

But nothing is impossible
The ground softens and slips out
from under your feet
and this time
there will be no forgiveness
No one will remember you
as anything more
than your last mistake

They will turn away
from the great wind
spinning you into
rags and trash
skittering fragmented
down the empty street
on your way out
to these waste spaces
covered in ash
where no one speaks
and no one remembers
you once had a name.

Since the Fall

I've lost the knack of vision.
These colors are not
what I remember,
nothing breathes or shimmers
the way it used to.
These woods might just as well
be tar and concrete,
there is no music
in the air and light.

I can't use your kindness.
The world is dead
and I am its widow
refusing to let go.

All the Wrong Moves

Once on a downtown street
I stood at the curb
and didn't know
how to read the signal light.
No memory, no automatic urge
rose to save me
and I froze, on the edge of a cliff
no one else could see.

Once on a bus
I knew the driver's bell
was not counting passengers,
but spelling out a secret plan
to my assigned assassin
and I had to get off the bus
before the bullets hit.

Under pressure
of the clever hidden threats
that could sniff me out
through all my best disguises,
I thought it best to hide
and sleep in my closet,
putting one more door
between me and whatever
had my scent.

But one small voice
spoke up clear and urgent
warning me I would not escape
my punishment
if I crossed that final line
and fled into the closet
one step too far past sane.

Unfit

after a Hausa Bird Headdress

She was an acre of tinder waiting for the match, would set her hair on fire and slap it out fast, a dramatic dare and rescue the wrong side of sane.

Followed by the smell of burning she marked everything she touched with fingerprints of ash.
She walked the alleys for hours. Those years most drinks came in glass bottles and every one she found she swung Hard and threw against a wall to hear it smash.
No one saw or stopped her and she left behind a trail of broken glass.

Trees spoke to her the way they speak to the deaf, in gestures and with the shapes of shadow and light splintering the air.
She knew each one she passed by its secret name, the path sap took from root to leaf, the way fog rested like a scarf around its shoulders, the way each day was a slow step in its long dance, the way they forgave her with new greens after each long winter's freeze.

She had no guardian angel but a great bird, a shadow falling like an owl, silent and dark, swift and accurate as any raptor, claw and beak and the hush of air coming down clean as a knife.
Even with that fierce eye, she was more crow than owl or eagle, no diva but a canny scavenger, polishing her darks in the sun, voice a raw caw, neither the gull's bold squawk nor the long soft grief of the dove, her voice unfit for words in any language but the one she invented to speak to herself.

Arms spread like wings she wore her fury like a crown, a totem, a warning, a bird whose silent scream could turn men's bones to sand, leaving her there at last a Queen, triumphant and alone.

Quick Fix/Emergency Room

I have no time for pride.
I have to pretend
nothing wrong has happened.
I did not come here
without manners,
my face burned off,
trying to breathe
around the pain,
begging for what I know
you'll never give.
I cannot say there was
even a flicker of derision
in the faces you turned to me,
but I can't imagine
greater humiliation-
even as the drug
took me into silence
I could feel your thoughts
moving behind the words
you used to hide them.

Dear Doctor

I came to you
in my extremity,
unfamiliar with the practical
limits of mercy.
The issue, you said,
was how it would look
if my pain could not be
contained
it would spoil your good
reputation.

If I was too sick, too suicidal,
too high risk, if I was likely
to succumb, and leave
a stain on your record

it would not go well for me
and I would have to take
all that pain
and all my hopes for help
away with me again.

Careful,
so careful
not to leave the smallest trace
of blood behind-
my footprints on your carpet
innocuous and brief enough
to fade.

Medication

Clears my head
damping me down until
all my noisy oppositions
go quiet and meek
and I grow calm
and sober as a gray
November day.
Good, you may think,
now we'll really
get things done.

But I can't help
remembering
what it was like
before my chemical
reformation
when every day
I wore carnival clothes
and thought
impossible things
going fast fast fast
as a bird's heartbeat,
as the quiver of an insect's
wing, as a rocket itching
to take off, as an engine
of desire, ready to win.

Bad Medicine

What you need
they said
is a good hard knock
upside the head
a clean break
it will leave you
with a lot less
to complain about

Afterward I kept still
as a white mouse
on a live wire grid
embarrassed
by rooms where every
thing waited
blank and innocent
knocked clean of meaning

And they were right
with so little left
there was not much
to complain of

I kept close
in the naked rooms
folding what rags
of memory I had
into smaller and smaller
packages

hoping if I hid them
well enough
I could keep them
after the white light
burned out everything

behind my eyelids
and they would be
the only colors left
in a world flat as a negative
where I had no complaints

Strangers So Unkind

Lined up on gurneys
by the elevator
we wait to be taken
downstairs where
they'll start IV's
and gel our temples
and strap the rubber
and metal crowns
to our heads
without once looking
any one of us
in the eye.
Then comes the whiff
of plastic and oxygen
as the mask comes down
and darkness rises
covering you like a lover
with a dark surprise
in his pocket.
You'll wake with a raging
headache and no
memory of anything much,
floating through the days
without leaving a trace
you could point to
and say, "This is mine."
You have lost your right
to time. Maybe someday you'll
remember this and
it won't be a nightmare
but I wouldn't
bet on it.

ECT the Curing

They crowned me in a cold room
and I was Queen of ice
Queen of the dark country
where morning never comes
Queen of blood and tears
and the dry grief
hungry for death
Queen of prisoners
bound and tied to her own
humiliation
waiting for the hour
of transubstantiation
waiting for the lightning
to find her
in her metal crown
to lift her
and burn her
and hang her
from Her own
illuminated bones
incinerating her name
leaving her empty
and ready for God
clean as a stone
when the ash of sacrifice is gone
and all her sins
have been forgotten
left behind with her life
before the lightning

Aftershock

Nothing can touch you
you wear an electric halo
that keeps you safe
from memory
you are made new again
clean as a baby
nothing can be your fault
you are a Saint
without a history
preparing to perform
your first miracles
you will be generous and blind
you will sniff out pain
like God's own bloodhound
you smile and your smile
leads you through the day
empty as the halls
you walk up and down
up and down
going nowhere
empty as your face
somehow still wet
with tears you didn't shed

After So Much ECT

My memory is pleated
like a fan or curtain
so much lost
in the folds between
one sharp crease and the next.
At best an uneven hopscotch
a tattered fabric
I wear with shame.
Talking to you
I skate over the cracks
fast so I won't fall in
I sing
so I don't stutter
and you won't get lost.
The worst is knowing
I was once continuous
unbroken
a long book
with no pages missing
a story anyone could read
without losing their way
even once.

After Shock

I came through calamity
calm and sure-footed
as any rope-walker
with an audience to please.
Now it's over I don't need
all that courage
and it's gone,
leaving me unsteady, strange
in a world I don't remember.

After combat, every soldier knows
it's hard to come home,
hard to believe
to an ordinary world.
After so many battles
I can't help waiting
for the next shell to hit,
can't help trying to avoid
the mines I know are there.

That Last Time in the Hospital

They took my nail file and pocket knife
and set someone there
on constant watch
in case I found the sudden
energy to act-
But I'd lost so much,
the flow of tears like blood
from an untended wound
diminished me
hour by hour
until I had
nothing to take me
from one night to the next.

I was too far away
for words to reach
that morning when the chaplain came.
Instead of prayer she took her violin
and played for us,
five people in a small room
all broken, stopped, defeated,
dumb with sorrow—

And music fell on us
like sweet rain,
a blessed absolution
outside the rules of pain.

The Madwoman as Apostate

Who refuses to confess
earning only the impatience
of contempt. Who is confused
by all the music
coming down at her
like a litany of everything
she keeps on getting wrong.
Who goes on without excuses
for her poor performance
her fumbles and missteps,
misreading all the cues,
standing when she should sit
speaking when she should sing
stumbling over every step
of even the simplest
celebrations. Who keeps
trying to get small enough
to get lost in the corners
to be overlooked and innocent
of catastrophe, still
trying to make the cut
the way she used to
easy and effortless,
but failing, fading, falling
farther and farther
into the airless room
with no furniture
and a locked door
and one small window
she can't look through-
She knows they can't see
anything but the Chimera
that has replaced her,

wrestled her down into a hold
she can't escape
telling her she must break
the world back out from under
the thick membrane
that stops her breath, deadly
and efficient as diphtheria-
though smashing glass won't
bring the colors back
or lift the sentence of despair,
just confirm the fright
she sees in faces
trying to assure her
she is not to blame
for this outrageous failure
that if she'd only stop
trying so hard
if only she'd be quiet
and stop crying
if only she'd settle down
to a smaller definition
wear her diagnosis
like a proper badge of shame
things would be better
and she'd feel so much lighter
free of rage and memory
unremarkable and tame.

Skins

Your repairs,
meant to heal,
wore me down
like sandpaper
reducing all my knots
and splintered edges
to a surface so bland
and smooth
no one would suspect
it had ever been anything
but innocuous.

Still I remember
that old skin
rough and graceless
marked by scars
and strange tattoos
like the autographs
of inquisitors
eager for confession.
Now I am domesticated
beyond suspicion
and I get no second glances
moving easily
among the wolves
perfect in this harmless
disguise.

Saving Face

After it's over
I'll count my spoons
and line the plates up
and swear no one ever
took anything from me
I wasn't ready to give.
If I do this well enough
I might even convince myself.
But I feel the cracks
spreading underneath
my fresh plaster,
and the pipes are leaking
somewhere in the cellar.
My thoughts needle me
with odd suspicions
and I can't dial down
my rampant swings
from grief to jubilation.
I don't think I'll get away
with my pretense
of order smooth as an egg
without a cloud or question
to mark its perfect surface.
I think I must go down
with all the other
tatterdemalions
too rough and raggedy
to let in the house,
to mad to expect
anything less.

Imposter

I don't know this woman
living in my house
doing everything
better than I did
speaking for me
using my voice
accepting all the compliments
I never got.
I dream of getting rid of her
cleverly and permanently.
I dream she goes away
without my help.
I wouldn't mind so much,
dear husband,
if you hadn't made her
so welcome.
Your sigh of relief
hurt more
than all her arrogance
and you are too content to see
she has erased me.

Ghost

I have survived myself
living on as a relic
of my own acts.
Such ghosts are lonely
they talk to themselves
and rearrange the furniture
all day long.
They can't remember
what it was like
to be alive,
but they know
they have lost everything
that matters.

The living dislike ghosts,
they are too chilly and uncomfortable,
with their burdens of penance
and regret, their oppressive
need to seem alive,
their eager hands
twisting and holding
onto nothing.

Resurrection is beyond me.
I can't bridge
that sudden dark
that separates us
from ourselves and each other
final as the word of God
who does not need us
to be complete.

Crow Song

It's too late to cooperate
or pretend I agree
with my own embarrassment
an old crow who still
steals shiny things
just because I like
their broken shapes
the lines of fracture
making sense
of what they wanted most
of how they failed
bright things broken

Like glass thrown
against a wall
falling in shards
of diamond
glittering beneath
the soles of boots
too thick to notice
how they shatter light
a million prisms
making rainbows
out of sacrifice

Call me thief, I only steal
what you would throw away
turn your back on
deaf to every raucous squawk
that raises an objection
refuses to obey
chooses its own splendor

its black and rusty
cape of feathers
before all your gaudy promises
ready for anyone
who keeps their head down
heart close, tongue
reined in, behaving
the way you think they should

Stolen

There is always something
more to lose.
Even when you think
you've been stripped
there's more to take:
gold teeth and fillings
fat and skin and bone,
your organs nested
in the flesh like gems
in velvet boxes.
You can't imagine
how thorough
these thieves can be.
When they are done
ransacking
you will be left
only a shadow
with nothing to show
for your pain.
Not even a word
traced in the fog
that hides your face
in the mirror,
not even a print
left like a signature
on something you once owned.

Vision

Once I had colors
twice as bright,
trees in the morning
called to me
like angels
dissolving into light.
I got entangled
in their shimmering
conversations,
lifted out of myself
by such sudden joys
I forgot what kept me
out of hope so long.
These intoxications
left me empty
unable to speak
or keep my feet square
on solid ground
walking in a straight line
as if nothing happened
and there were no miracles
here for anyone
with eyes to see.

Enthralled

for my sister, who always knew me, and never let me go

I found myself lost
black, mechanical,
an alien left behind.
I had razor blades
instead of bones
beneath my skin.
I spoke in colors
words like sequins
breaking light
into smaller and smaller
fractions.
I had to sort you out
between the voices
of the trees, the grass
shouting and singing
sharp and dangerous
as fields of broken glass.
I came naked
feathered and spurred
my tongue baroque
unregulated,
my arms full
of awkward gifts:
apologies like small
black holes
swallowing worlds
blind spots white
as lepers
running fevers and other
sudden lightnings
hard to find room for
in any reasonable space.

But you held fast
through fire season,
keeping track
while I burned and raved,
a speed demon
racing through a thousand
changing shapes.
You held strong
laying claim
against enchantment.
You never blinked,
never saw
any face but mine,
rock steady,
waiting for me
underneath the shadow maze
of strange mutations
where I found myself
lost.

Your Apology, Dear Friend

Even if it came today
would be too late.
I've had too long to remember
how you saw, and turned away,
how even the smallest space
was more than I could take
in your good life, already full,
and rich with nothing out of place.
There was no room in you for grace,
to see my awkward, mad mistakes
as small faults, and no cause to flee
in fear that you might share my fate.
Such grief is not contagious—
you were always safe.

Invitation

Come to me
when you have wrestled
with the angel
no one else can see,
when nightmare stalks you
in the daylit street
and you go dark
as a bulb one turn
too loose.

Come to me
when the road twists
into knots you can't resolve
and the faces you see
stare coldly out
of stiffened masks
with painted smiles
and sharp teeth
flashing as they pass.

Come to me
when you have forgotten
how to read
when all you see
are turned backs
and raised eyebrows
when you've gone outside the lines
of every map you had.

Come to me
when you speak words of fire
that burn your tongue
and turn to ashes on the air.

Come to me
when you wear death's kiss
like a badge on your body
and hear his voice inside you
intimate and constant
as your own heart beat.

Come to me
when nothing's left
to look at all familiar

and I will meet you there

About the Author

Mary McCarthy is a retired Registered Nurse who has always been a writer and artist. Her work has appeared in many journals and anthologies, including *The Ekphrastic World,* edited by Lorette Luzajic; *The Plague Papers,* edited by Robbi Nester; and recent issues of *Earth's Daughters, 3rd Wednesday, Caustic Frolic, Verse Virtual,* and *Gyroscope.* She has been a Pushcart and Best of the Net nominee. She has also had a lifelong struggle with Bipolar illness, experiencing all that means in terms of work, career, relationships, and identity. Even now, this is unsettled territory, filled with sudden obstacles, surprises, trials and occasional blessings.

www.ingramcontent.com/pod-product-compliance
Lightning Source LLC
Chambersburg PA
CBHW030915170426
43193CB00009BA/851